W9-BLV-412

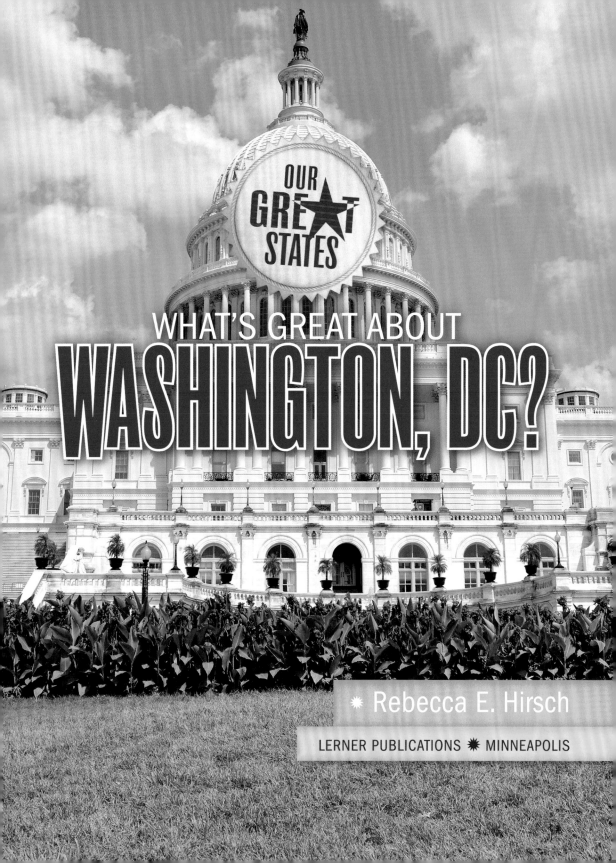

OUR
GRE★T
STATES

WHAT'S GREAT ABOUT

WASHINGTON, DC?

✸ Rebecca E. Hirsch

LERNER PUBLICATIONS ✸ MINNEAPOLIS

CONTENTS

Copyright © 2015
by Lerner Publishing Group, Inc.

Content Consultant: Chris Myers Asch, Editor,
Washington History

All rights reserved. International copyright
secured. No part of this book may be
reproduced, stored in a retrieval system, or
transmitted in any form or by any means—
electronic, mechanical, photocopying,
recording, or otherwise—without the prior
written permission of Lerner Publishing
Group, Inc., except for the inclusion of brief
quotations in an acknowledged review.

Lerner Publications Company
A division of Lerner Publishing Group, Inc.
241 First Avenue North
Minneapolis, MN 55401 USA

For reading levels and more information, look
up this title at www.lernerbooks.com.

Main body text set in ITC Franklin Gothic Std
Book Condensed 12/15.
Typeface provided by Adobe Systems.

Library of Congress Cataloging-in-Publication
Data

Hirsch, Rebecca E.
    What's great about Washington, DC? /
by Rebecca E. Hirsch.
        pages   cm. – (Our great states)
    Includes index.
    ISBN 978-1-4677-3859-0 (lib. bdg. :
alk. paper)
    ISBN 978-1-4677-6083-6 (pbk.)
    ISBN 978-1-4677-6261-8 (EB pdf)
    1. Washington (D.C.)—Guidebooks—
Juvenile literature. I. Title.
F192.3.H56 2015
975.3—dc23   2014024557

Manufactured in the United States of America
1 – PC – 12/31/14

WASHINGTON, DC, Welcomes You!

Washington, DC, is the nation's capital. In this world-class city, US history comes to life. The city is home to the White House, the Capitol, and the Supreme Court. Residents of Washington, DC, love to get outdoors and have fun. You'll see people biking, running, walking, and kayaking on the Potomac River. From the National Mall to the National Zoo, there is so much to see and do here. Keep reading to discover ten things that make Washington, DC, great!

MARYLAND

MARYLAND

Reno Reservoir
(410 feet/125 m)

Chesapeake & Ohio Canal

Potomac River

Georgetown

N

US National
Arboretum

NATIONAL
MALL

Tidal
Basin

WASHINGTON
CHANNEL

Anacostia River

VIRGINIA

Potomac River

Miles
0   1   2
0   1   2   3
Kilometers

Explore Washington, DC's monuments and all the places in between. Just turn the page to find out all about the NATION'S CAPITAL. >

Watch orangutans walk across wires above the National Zoo walkways.

NATIONAL ZOO

> Start your visit to the nation's capital at the National Zoo. It's free! And it is a great place to see endangered animals from all around the world. Elephants, tigers, and zebras roam the zoo's grounds. Head to the middle of the zoo to Lemur Island. The lemurs like to sunbathe in the morning sun. Watch them sit upright to sun their furry white bellies. Meet the orangutans at the Great Ape House. See them walk on wires above the zoo walkways!

Then stop by the panda house. Don't miss the American Trail. You'll find animals from North America. Watch the otters swim and play, and let the sea lions entertain you. They love to play with visitors! After you're done visiting the animals, take a ride on the carousel. Ride on statues of animals you just saw, including pandas and zebras. You can even choose to ride on a Komodo dragon!

THE DISTRICT OF COLUMBIA

Washington, DC, is not a state. It is a special district. It was created to be the home of our national government. *DC* stands for "District of Columbia." More than six hundred thousand people live in DC. Each state in the country has two senators and at least one representative in the House. DC has no senators. Its delegate in the House of Representatives cannot vote on issues. Many people in DC think that is unfair.

The Abraham Lincoln statue at Lincoln Memorial stands 19 feet (6 m) tall.

NATIONAL MALL

> After visiting the animals, head over to see some of the nation's most famous statues. The National Mall is a 2-mile-long (3-kilometer) park. It stretches from the US Capitol to the Lincoln Memorial. Some important events in history took place here. This is where Martin Luther King Jr. gave his famous "I Have a Dream" speech in 1963.

Bring a kite to fly, or toss a Frisbee. Or just relax on the grass. There's plenty of room to spread out a blanket. Have a picnic on one of the world's most famous lawns. Then visit the Washington Monument. You can't miss it. It rises 555 feet (169 meters) into the air. Rocket to the top of the monument in the high-speed elevator. See a bird's-eye view of the city from the top. Next, head to the Lincoln Memorial. Climb the steps and gaze up at a statue of America's sixteenth president, Abraham Lincoln. You'll find two of Lincoln's most famous speeches engraved on the wall.

"I HAVE A DREAM"
On August 28, 1963, 250,000 people filled the National Mall. They were gathered for the March on Washington. This was the largest civil rights demonstration in history. Many civil rights leaders spoke that day. Martin Luther King Jr. spoke last. He delivered his famous "I Have a Dream" speech. In this speech, he talked about his dream of equality and justice for people of all races.

NATIONAL CHERRY BLOSSOM FESTIVAL

> In late March and early April, thousands of Japanese cherry trees bloom in Washington, DC. A huge festival celebrates the gift of Washington, DC's first cherry trees. The mayor of Tokyo, Japan, gave three thousand of the trees to the city in 1912. Cherry trees line the Tidal Basin. This reservoir lies between the Potomac River and the Washington Channel. Rent a paddleboat and see the cherry trees from the water. Spot the Jefferson Memorial and the Washington Monument from your boat. Don't miss the Cherry Blossom Festival Parade! You'll see colorful floats and marching bands.

Celebrate the festival by flying a kite. The sky over the National Mall fills with thousands of kites during the Blossom Kite Festival. See sport kites perform amazing tricks. Fighter kites battle one another in the sky. Bring your own kite to fly. Or visit the activity tents to make your own. You can also get lessons from experienced fliers.

View the National Cherry Blossom Festival while paddleboating in the Tidal Basin.

Watch giant helium balloons float past at the Cherry Blossom Parade.

NATIONAL MUSEUM OF NATURAL HISTORY

> The nation's capital is known for amazing museums. One of the most exciting is the National Museum of Natural History. It is the most visited museum in the country. You'll find this free museum on the National Mall. In the rotunda, you can see the largest land animal. The 14-foot-tall (4 m) African elephant looms above visitors. It weighs a massive 8 tons (7 metric tons).

Next, head to the Hall of Mammals. You'll get an up-close look at stuffed tigers, gorillas, and polar bears. Then come face-to-face with ancient humans in the Hall of Human Origins. Do you like insects? If so, the Insect Zoo is the place for you! See giant hissing cockroaches. Or watch a colony of leaf-cutter ants at work. Surround yourself with butterflies in the Butterfly Pavilion.

Stand next to and compare yourself to stuffed mammals in the National Museum of Natural History's Hall of Mammals.

PIERRE CHARLES L'ENFANT

The nation's first president, George Washington, asked French engineer Pierre Charles L'Enfant to design the new capital of the United States. L'Enfant wanted to create a beautiful city. He wanted it to be a shining symbol of democracy. His plan included wide streets and circular parks. It also had a grand avenue, later called the National Mall. At the center of L'Enfant's design was the Capitol. Several diagonal streets meet at the Capitol. They represent rays of light shining out from the home of our government.

See the Oval Office, the official office of the US president, on your tour of the White House.

THE WHITE HOUSE

> Next, tour the world's most famous house. There are no tour guides in the White House, but guards will answer your questions. Visit the State Dining Room to see where the president of the United States eats his meals. Peek out the windows for amazing views of the National Mall. Just remember, you must request a tour weeks or months in advance. Contact your state's Congress member for more information.

Stop in at the White House Visitor Center. You'll see exhibits about the presidents and first ladies who lived there. You can also watch a video about the history of the White House. Be sure to pick up a *Junior Ranger Activity Guide*. It's filled with fun facts. Did you know President Benjamin Harrison was afraid of the first electric lights in the White House? He hired an electrician to turn the lights on and off for him!

Looking for a bite to eat? Head to one of Washington's oldest saloons. Old Ebbitt Grill is just a short walk from the White House. This restaurant has been a favorite of many US presidents. Step inside for a blast from the past. Gas-powered chandeliers light the dark wood booths. Enjoy a burger or a plate of piping hot macaroni and cheese.

THE BURNING OF THE WHITE HOUSE

During the War of 1812, the United States fought Great Britain. British troops burned the White House in 1814. President James Madison and First Lady Dolley Madison had already fled to Maryland. The war ended six months later, and the White House was rebuilt. President James Monroe returned home to the new White House in 1817.

CAPITOL HILL

> Feel US history come alive on Capitol Hill. Capitol Hill is formally known as the US Capitol. This beautiful building is the home of the US Congress. Head to the Capitol Visitor Center for a tour. Be sure to look up in the rotunda. Its dome ceiling is 180 feet (55 m) high. At the top, you'll see intricate designs and a painting. Can you tell which president is in the middle of the painting? Next, step into the National Statuary Hall. Try to find the spot where you can hear a person whisper from all the way across the room. Test out for yourself how John Quincy Adams used to eavesdrop on conversations.

After your tour, visit the US Botanic Garden. You can even help care for the plants and flowers! Grab a shovel or a watering can, and get to work. Walk through a tropical rain forest with a waterfall and a stream. Pick up a *Family Field Journal.* You can make notes and draw pictures of the plants and flowers you see.

THE NATION'S CAPITAL

When Thomas Jefferson wrote the Declaration of Independence in 1776, the city of Washington, DC, did not exist. Congress gave President George Washington the right to choose a new capital of the country. In 1790, Washington selected the location for the capital, which was named in his honor. He chose land on either side of the Potomac River. The land had been part of Maryland and Virginia. For ten years, enslaved African Americans and other workers built the city. Washington officially became the US capital on December 1, 1800.

Smell and touch the many plants in the US Botanic Garden.

US NATIONAL ARBORETUM

> Do you like exploring the outdoors? You'll find 450 acres (182 hectares) to roam at the US National Arboretum. Hike through woods and cross wooden bridges. Find magical spots to hide among the trees at this living museum. For a real treat, play around the National Capitol Columns in the Ellipse Meadow. These giant columns were once part of the US Capitol. They were taken down and moved in 1958 when new columns replaced them.

Search around the arboretum. Can you find the biggest tree? Try stretching your arms around it. Good luck! This enormous willow oak tree has been growing since before the Civil War (1861–1865). Next, try to find the oldest tree. It's in the National Bonsai & Penjing Museum. There you can learn how bonsai artists create miniature versions of real trees. Head to the Grove of State Trees. You'll find trees from all fifty states.

The National Capitol Columns, originally part of the US Capitol, were built in 1828.

The US National Arboretum is the perfect place to enjoy a picnic.

INTERNATIONAL SPY MUSEUM

> Become a secret spy at the International Spy Museum. You won't be alone. Washington, DC, is home to more spies than anywhere else in the world. At the museum, you'll start by choosing your secret identity. Choose which disguises you want to wear. Then play the part of your new identity as you sneak through the exhibits. Put your secret agent skills to the test. Crack a spy code. Listen in on secret conversations. Crawl through an air duct while trying to keep quiet. Can you find another agent in disguise?

Be sure to check out the School for Spies. You can see invisible ink and cleverly disguised weapons. Learn how spies create secret disguises. As you wrap up your visit, there is one final test: Just how well did you keep your cover as a secret spy?

See a shoe rigged with a microphone and other spy gadgets at the International Spy Museum.

Choose your own spy identity and disguise at the International Spy Museum.

NATIONALS PARK

> Spring and summer are time for baseball! Watch the Washington Nationals play at Nationals Park. This exciting ballpark opened in 2008. Zoom to Nationals Park on the Metro. It's the city's subway system. A subway stop is just half a block from the stadium. Be sure to take in the great view from the ballpark. Can you see the Washington Monument? On nongame days, you can take a tour of the stadium. Visit the dugouts. Then throw out a pitch.

On game days, get to the stadium early. Some of your favorite players will sign autographs. Don't forget to bring your glove. You might catch a foul ball! Can you spot Screech the eagle? He's the team mascot. Watch him flutter across the field! Then root for your favorite among the president mascots as they race around the field. Will Washington, Jefferson, Lincoln, Teddy Roosevelt, or Taft come in first?

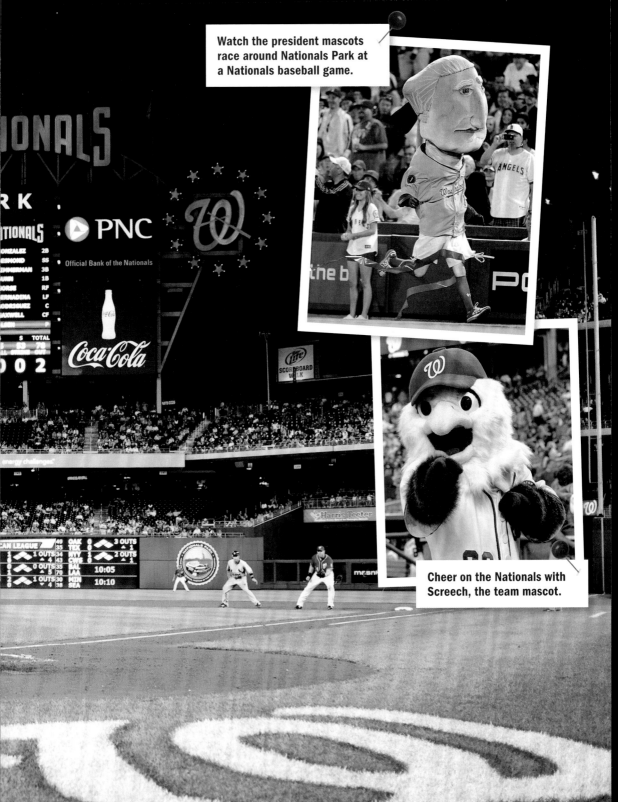

Watch the president mascots race around Nationals Park at a Nationals baseball game.

Cheer on the Nationals with Screech, the team mascot.

Paddle down the Potomac River in a canoe or a kayak.

GEORGETOWN

> End your trip by heading to Washington, DC's oldest neighborhood. Georgetown has been a lively place since before the Revolutionary War (1775–1783). George Washington and Thomas Jefferson both walked these streets.

First, visit the Chesapeake & Ohio Canal. This waterway was built by workers and once provided transportation. You can ride in a canal boat pulled by a mule, just as people did in the 1800s. Ropes connect the mules with the boat. The mules walk on a boardwalk beside the canal to pull the boat. Guides dressed in period clothing will tell you what life was like back then.

Then find more outdoor fun along the Potomac River. Bike the Capital Crescent Trail. The fountain at Georgetown Waterfront Park will cool you off after all of your activities.

Cruise along the Chesapeake & Ohio Canal as mules pull your canal boat.

YOUR TOP TEN

You have read about ten exciting things to see and do in Washington, DC. Now imagine you are planning a trip to Washington, DC. What would your top ten list include? What would you like to see and do in the nation's capital city? Grab a sheet of paper and make your top ten list. Try turning your list into a book. You can illustrate it with your own drawings or pictures from the Internet or magazines.

WASHINGTON, DC, BY MAP

> MAP KEY

⊛ Capital city

○ City

◎ Point of interest

▲ Highest elevation

—·— District border

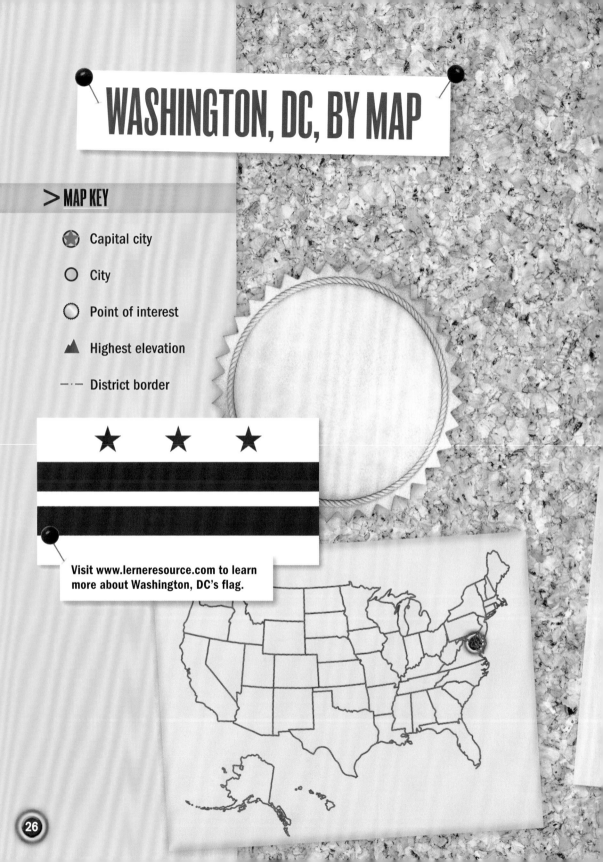

Visit www.lerneresource.com to learn more about Washington, DC's flag.

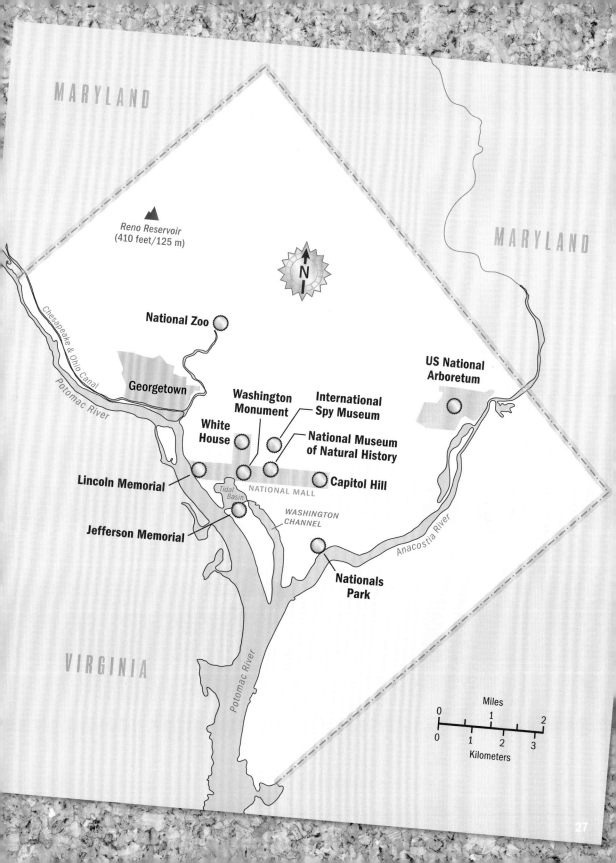

MARYLAND

Reno Reservoir
(410 feet/125 m)

MARYLAND

N

Chesapeake & Ohio Canal

Potomac River

National Zoo

US National
Arboretum

Georgetown

Washington
Monument

International
Spy Museum

White
House

National Museum
of Natural History

Lincoln Memorial

Tidal
Basin

NATIONAL MALL

Capitol Hill

WASHINGTON
CHANNEL

Jefferson Memorial

Anacostia River

Nationals
Park

VIRGINIA

Potomac River

Miles

0   1   2

0   1   2   3

Kilometers

WASHINGTON, DC, FACTS

NICKNAME: DC

SONG: "The Star-Spangled Banner"

MOTTO: *Justitia Omnibus*, or "Justice to All"

> **FLOWER:** American beauty rose

TREE: scarlet oak

> **BIRD:** wood thrush

DATE ESTABLISHED: September 9, 1791

AREA: 68 square miles (176 sq. km)

AVERAGE JANUARY TEMPERATURE: 34°F (1°C)

AVERAGE JULY TEMPERATURE: 80°F (27°C)

POPULATION: 646,449 (2013)

NUMBER OF US CONGRESS MEMBERS: 1 nonvoting representative; 0 senators

NUMBER OF ELECTORAL VOTES: 3

MAJOR INDUSTRIES: government, legal, medical service, tourism, printing and publishing

> **HOLIDAYS AND CELEBRATIONS:** National Cherry Blossom Festival

GLOSSARY

arboretum: a place where trees and plants are grown for scientific research and education

canal: an artificial waterway for boats

Capitol: the building in which the US Congress meets

civil rights: the personal freedoms of a US citizen

democracy: a form of government in which the people choose their leaders in elections

endangered: at risk of disappearing forever

mascot: a person, animal, or object that represents a group and is said to bring good luck

rain forest: a hot, thick woodland that receives a lot of rain and has very tall trees

reservoir: a lake built by workers that stores water

rotunda: a large round room often covered by a dome

Supreme Court: the highest court in the United States

LERNER

SOURCE

Expand learning beyond the printed book. Download free, complementary educational resources for this book from our website, www.lerneresource.com.

FURTHER INFORMATION

House, Katherine L. *The White House for Kids*. Chicago: Chicago Review Press, 2014. Find out what it's like to live and work in the most famous house in the country.

National Museum of Natural History: Vertebrate Paleo Team Fieldwork
http://paleobiology.si.edu/dinosaurs/collection/labs/vpLab/index.html
Get a behind-the-scenes tour of how paleontologists prepare dinosaur fossils.

National Zoo: Meet Our Animals
http://nationalzoo.si.edu/Animals/default.cfm
See photos and learn cool facts about the animals that live at the National Zoo.

Nelson, Robin, and Sandy Donovan. *The Congress: A Look at the Legislative Branch*. Minneapolis: Lerner Publications, 2012. Check out this book to learn more about the US Congress and how it works.

Ogintz, Eileen. *The Kid's Guide to Washington, DC*. Guilford, CT: GPP Travel, 2013. Use this book to help you plan your trip to Washington, DC.

The United States National Arboretum: Arboretum Virtual Tour for Kids
http://www.usna.usda.gov/Gardens/collections/VirtualTours
/KidsVirtualTour_02.html#Slide
Check out weird and wonderful plants and places at the US National Arboretum with this virtual tour.

INDEX

PHOTO ACKNOWLEDGMENTS

The images in this book are used with the permission of: © Orhan Cam/Shutterstock Images, pp. 1, 4–5, 7, 16–17, 24; NASA, pp. 2–3; © Laura Westlund/Independent Picture Service, pp. 5 (top), 27; © EastVillage Images/ Shutterstock Images, pp. 5 (bottom), 16; Carol M. Highsmith/Library of Congress, pp. 6–7 (LC-HS503-5064), 12–13 (LC-HS503-2082), 13 (bottom) (LC-HS503-4643), 19 (top) (LC-DIG-highsm-10452), 24–25 (LC-HS503-6566); © Konstantin L/Shutterstock Images, p. 6; © ExaMedia Photography/Shutterstock Images, pp. 8–9; © Tupungato/Shutterstock Images, p. 8 (top); © Everett Collection Historical/Alamy, p. 8 (bottom); © Songquan Deng/Shutterstock Images, pp. 10–11; © Lissandra Melo/ Shutterstock Images, p. 11 (top); © Shutterstock Images, pp. 11 (bottom), 28; Daderot, p. 13 (top); © Vacclav/Shutterstock Images, pp. 14–15; © Chuck Aghoian/Shutterstock Images, p. 14; National Archives and Records Administration, p. 15; © Ilene MacDonald/Alamy, p. 17; © Jon Bilous/Shutterstock Images, pp. 18–19; © FernandoMadeira/Shutterstock Images, p. 19 (bottom); © Richard T. Nowitz/Corbis, pp. 20–21; © Chuck Kennedy/KRT/Newscom, p. 21 (bottom); © Bill Kotsatos/Polaris/Newscom, p. 21 (top); © David Coleman/Alamy, pp. 22–23; © Zuma Press, Inc/Alamy, p. 23 (top); © Mark Goldman/Icon SMI/Corbis, p. 23 (bottom); © Spirit of America/ Shutterstock Images, p. 25; © liangpv/ iStockphoto, p. 26; © Dudaeva/Shutterstock Images, p. 29 (top); © Paul Reeves Photography/ Shutterstock Images, p. 29 (bottom).

Cover: © Howard Nevitt, Jr./Dreamstime.com (panda); © Raymond Boyd/Michael Ochs Archives/Getty Images (spy museum); © iStockphoto.com/dszc, (tidal basin); Carol M. Highsmith's America, Library of Congress, Prints and Photographs Division LC-DIG-highsm-04492, (Capitol); © Laura Westlund/Independent Picture Service (map); © iStockphoto.com/fpm (seal); © iStockphoto.com/vicm (pushpins); © iStockphoto.com/benz190 (corkboard).

KIRKWOOD

5/4/2015

J 975.3 HIRSCH
Hirsch, Rebecca E.
What's great about Washington, DC? /
R2002706279 KIRKWD

Atlanta-Fulton Public Library